GAO United States
General Accounting Office
Washington, D.C. 20548

General Government Division

AF730596

B-253639

October 8, 1993

The Honorable J.J. Pickle
Chairman, Subcommittee on Oversight
Committee on Ways and Means
House of Representatives

Dear Mr. Chairman:

This report responds to your request that we determine whether (1) IRS' classification of certain accounts as currently not collectible is appropriate and (2) IRS' efforts to monitor these accounts for future collection potential are adequate. It focuses on individual taxpayer accounts that have been classified currently not collectible because taxpayers were unable to pay their delinquencies or IRS was unable to locate or contact them. The report contains recommendations to the Commissioner of Internal Revenue on ways to improve the currently not collectible determination, monitoring, reactivation, and oversight processes.

As arranged with the Subcommittee, unless you publicly announce its contents earlier, we plan no further distribution of this report until 30 days from the date of this letter. At that time, we will send copies to the Commissioner of Internal Revenue, the Secretary of the Treasury, and other interested parties. We will also make copies available to others upon request.

Major contributors are listed in appendix IV. If you have any questions about this report, please call me at (202) 512-5407.

Sincerely yours,

Jennie S. Stathis

Jennie S. Stathis
Director, Tax Policy and
Administration Issues

Executive Summary

Purpose

The amount of delinquent taxes on the Internal Revenue Service's (IRS) records is growing and so is the amount classified as currently not collectible (CNC). At the end of fiscal year 1992, IRS' inventory of individual and business delinquent accounts totaled $130.6 billion. Because of overstatements in the inventory, the total does not reflect the true amount of delinquent taxes owed. IRS had classified as CNC and thereby suspended collection action on accounts totaling $52.4 billion, or 40 percent of the inventory. During fiscal year 1992, IRS classified over 1.2 million accounts totaling $9.5 billion as CNC. Unless the taxpayers make voluntary payments or claim refunds that IRS can offset, most of the CNC amounts will never be collected.

Because of the large amount of recorded CNC tax debt and the potential revenue losses, the Chairman of the Subcommittee on Oversight, House Committee on Ways and Means, requested that GAO determine whether IRS' CNC determinations were appropriate and whether IRS' efforts to monitor CNC accounts for future collection potential were adequate. This report focuses on individual taxpayer accounts that IRS classified as CNC because of the individuals' financial hardship or because IRS was unable to locate or contact the taxpayers. These accounts make up about 90 percent of the total dollar amount of individual CNC accounts.

Background

IRS collects delinquent taxes through a three-stage process consisting of written notices, telephone calls, and personal contacts. At any stage, IRS can classify an account as CNC if the taxpayer cannot be located or contacted, payment would cause significant financial hardship on the taxpayer, the taxpayer is bankrupt, a business taxpayer no longer exists, or an individual taxpayer is deceased. CNC determinations require IRS supervisory approval, and a sample of cases are subject to IRS quality reviews.

IRS monitors tax returns filed by taxpayers with CNC accounts to determine whether collection potential has improved sufficiently for IRS to resume collection action. In addition, IRS sends annual reminder notices to taxpayers with CNC accounts and offsets any refunds these taxpayers claim on subsequent tax returns.

IRS has initiatives underway that could affect the number of CNC accounts. For example, IRS is making it easier for taxpayers to settle their tax debts for amounts less than the amounts owed, and IRS is expanding its use of installment agreements.

GAO reviewed 107 randomly selected individual taxpayer accounts that were classified as CNC during August and September 1991 in 5 IRS district offices. GAO also randomly selected, from IRS' national database of CNC accounts as of June 1991, a sample of 100 individual CNC accounts classified as unable to pay and analyzed the 1990 tax returns of the 52 taxpayers in the sample who had filed them.

Results in Brief

IRS is losing the potential of collecting hundreds of millions of dollars because of its CNC determination, oversight, and monitoring processes. GAO found CNC determinations that were based on inadequate work, were questionable given the available information, or did not fully provide for future collection potential. GAO found that IRS did not provide its employees with specific guidance to make CNC determinations, and IRS' supervisory reviews and postreviews were not identifying and correcting problems with CNC determinations. Some of these determinations allowed taxpayers who reported incomes of more than $70,000 to pay nothing towards their tax debts when installment payments may have been more appropriate.

GAO also found accounts that may not have been collectible at the time they were classified as CNC but, at the time of GAO's review, had collection potential that was not being realized because collection action remained suspended. Some accounts had not been reactivated because of IRS' policy of not reevaluating collection potential during the first 65 weeks after an account is classified as CNC—referred to as the reactivation hold period.

Other accounts had not been reactivated because IRS tracks only one taxpayer when monitoring a joint CNC account and had therefore not been aware of the potential of collecting from the other taxpayer. In addition, some of these accounts were ignored because IRS' reactivation criteria did not consider all indicators of collection potential. GAO noted that even when CNC accounts are reactivated, IRS still may not realize potential collections because of its inefficient collection practices for reactivated accounts.

Unless IRS improves its CNC determination and monitoring processes, it will continue to forgo potential collections.

Principal Findings

Inadequate and Questionable CNC Determinations

GAO identified inadequate or questionable actions in an estimated 55 percent of the 1,233 accounts classified as CNC in 5 IRS districts during August and September 1991. GAO found inadequate reviews of taxpayers' financial status, including unquestioned acceptance of what taxpayers considered necessary living expenses, computations that excluded some income, and failures to follow asset and address leads. For example, in 12 percent of the unable to pay cases, IRS allowed as necessary living expenses unverified and questionable expenses, such as unreasonably large mortgage payments, expenses for three cars, payments for costly vehicle leases, and payments on substantial amounts of unsecured debt. These inadequate or questionable determination actions allowed some taxpayers earning more than $70,000 a year to pay nothing towards their tax debts when installment payments may have been more appropriate.

In an estimated 22 percent of the unable to pay cases, IRS did not adequately provide for future collection potential because it did not file liens on delinquent taxpayers' property or it established reactivation income levels that, on the basis of the taxpayers' provided expenses, were much higher than needed to cover the taxpayers' expenses and allow for some tax payments. These problems appear to be caused by the subjective criteria used to make the CNC determination and oversight mechanisms—supervisory and postreviews—that are allowing inappropriate CNC determinations to occur. In addition, postreviews are not providing the type of information that would lead to needed procedural changes to help eliminate inappropriate CNC determinations. (See pp. 21 through 28.)

CNC Monitoring Limitations

Limitations on IRS' CNC monitoring process have also resulted in lost collection potential. On the basis of an analysis of over 300,000 individual taxpayer accounts classified as CNC as of July 1991, GAO found that almost 36,000 of the unable to pay accounts, totaling about $250 million, would have been reactivated had IRS' 65-week hold period not prevented reactivation. These taxpayers had filed returns with incomes above the levels IRS had established for reactivation. In addition, IRS tracks only one taxpayer when monitoring a joint CNC account. Thus, IRS loses the potential to collect from the other taxpayer if separate returns are filed after the CNC determination. In an estimated 12 percent of the cases GAO reviewed in five districts, taxpayers separated after a joint liability was classified as CNC. Further, GAO found instances in which IRS' reliance on income as the sole reactivation criterion prevented reactivation when other assets were available that could have been used as collection sources. (See pp. 30 through 36.)

Inefficient Collection Practices

IRS also impedes its ability to make collections from reactivated CNC accounts by treating these accounts as new delinquencies. Although these taxpayers already know they owe the tax debts and have gone through the collection process, IRS may start the notice process all over again. This process consists of sending notices to the taxpayer and can take up to 6 months. Also, staff working a reactivated account rarely have the original case file and thus do not have the benefit of the earlier investigation to identify changes in the taxpayer's financial condition. (See p. 33.)

Recommendations

GAO recommends that the Commissioner of Internal Revenue take the following actions:

- Establish guidelines for determining taxpayers' ability to pay delinquent tax debts, including selecting income levels at which CNC accounts will be reactivated. IRS needs criteria for allowable expenses in total or by category that would require, except in extraordinary situations, at least minimum payments from delinquent taxpayers with incomes above a specific level. (See pp. 28 and 29.)
- Ensure that oversight mechanisms—supervisory and postreviews—are thorough enough to identify inappropriate CNC determinations and that reporting standards are developed to provide meaningful information that can be used to identify problems needing IRS-wide corrective action. (See p. 41.)
- Eliminate the 65-week reactivation hold period, track both taxpayers when they file separately but have joint CNC delinquencies, use all available indicators of collection potential as reactivation criteria, and expedite the collection process for reactivated accounts. (See p. 34.)

Agency Comments

In an August 5, 1993, letter commenting on a draft of this report (see app. III), the Commissioner of Internal Revenue agreed that the CNC area could be improved and concurred at least in principle with most of the report recommendations. Most significantly, the Commissioner promised actions to address the issue of lifestyle choices and committed to long-term improvement in the quality of CNC accounts. "While the IRS will not dictate lifestyle choices to a taxpayer, the expectation will exist that high income taxpayers ... [will] resolve their tax obligations."

The Commissioner did not agree with eliminating the 65-week reactivation hold because it ensured that cases were not reactivated unnecessarily when the taxpayers' income was already considered during the investigation. However, as GAO pointed out, the hold also precluded the timely reactivation of other accounts. Thus, GAO continues to believe that some change is necessary to ensure the timely reactivation of cases based on future income that was not considered during the CNC investigation.

Detailed comments and GAO's evaluations are included at the end of chapters 2, 3, and 4 of the report.

Contents

Abbreviations

ACS	Automated Collection System
CNC	Currently Not Collectible
CQMS	Collection Quality Measurement System
IRM	Internal Revenue Manual
IRS	Internal Revenue Service

Chapter 1

Introduction

The amount of delinquent federal taxes in the Internal Revenue Service's (IRS) accounts receivable inventory has increased greatly over the past decade. At the end of fiscal year 1992, IRS' gross accounts receivable inventory totaled $130.6 billion,[1] of which $52.4 billion, or 40 percent, was classified as currently not collectible (CNC). IRS classifies accounts as CNC and thereby suspends collection action when it determines that collection from the taxpayer is not currently possible. CNC accounts have been one of the fastest growing and the largest component of the accounts receivable inventory. In fiscal year 1992, IRS classified as CNC over 1.2 million delinquent accounts totaling $9.5 billion in assessments.[2]

Concerned about the collection of delinquent taxes, the Subcommittee on Oversight, House Committee on Ways and Means, requested that we review the CNC portion of the accounts receivable inventory to determine whether the accounts are properly classified and whether IRS efforts to monitor CNC accounts for future collection potential are adequate. This report deals with individual accounts that IRS classified as CNC because taxpayers were unable to pay their delinquencies or IRS was unable to locate or contact them. We concentrated on this portion of the CNC inventory because it had the most potential for additional collections.[3] As figure 1.1 shows, as of September 30, 1992, individual accounts classified as CNC for these reasons contained about 90 percent of the individual CNC account assessments.

[1]The gross accounts receivable inventory includes individual and business accounts. Because of overstatements in the inventory, gross accounts receivable does not reflect the amount of delinquent taxes owed. In addition, IRS will not be able to collect much of the portion of the inventory that is owed, primarily because delinquent taxpayers cannot pay or IRS cannot find them.

[2]Some IRS statistics were available only for assessed delinquencies and did not include additional accrued interest and penalties. Assessed amounts include the unpaid taxes as well as interest and penalties that are due at the time IRS establishes an account. Additional interest and penalties continue to accrue after the account is established. Unless otherwise noted, the statistics used in this report include accrued interest and penalties.

[3]Business CNC accounts largely pertain to bankrupt and defunct corporations and hold little collection potential.

Figure 1.1: Reasons for the Individual CNC Account Assessments in the September 30, 1992, Accounts Receivable Inventory

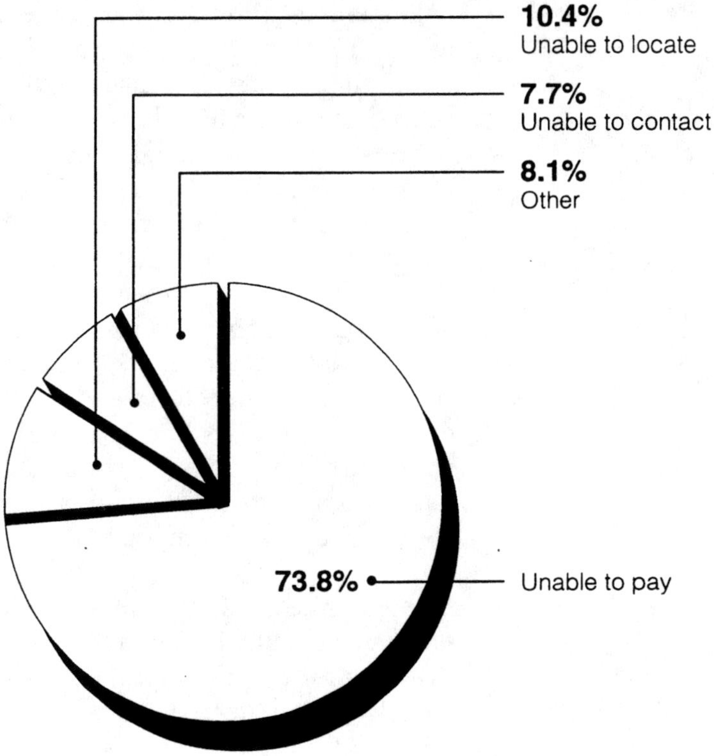

Note: The percentages indicate the portion of total individual CNC account assessments attributable to each reason.

Source: IRS data.

Process for Collecting Delinquent Taxes

IRS uses a three-stage process to collect delinquent taxes. In the first stage, IRS service centers mail delinquent taxpayers a series of computer-generated notices (bills) demanding payment. The final notice is sent by registered mail and is a notice of IRS' intent to levy.[4] During the notice process, IRS responds to any taxpayer replies. Unresolved delinquencies over certain dollar thresholds are transferred to the second stage, called the Automated Collection System (ACS).

Collection employees use ACS to telephone delinquent taxpayers, receive calls from taxpayers, and retrieve information from taxpayer accounts.

[4]A levy is the seizure of a taxpayer's property (or rights to property), including assets in the possession of employers and financial institutions, such as wages and bank deposits.

During this stage, Collection employees attempt to collect the delinquencies through payment arrangements or levies. If delinquencies are not resolved in ACS, they are placed in a computerized holding file called the "queue" and assigned to revenue officers in one of the 63 district offices according to collection potential. In this third stage, revenue officers attempt personal contact with taxpayers; search internal and external sources for taxpayers' assets; initiate levies; and seize taxpayers' physical property, such as automobiles and homes, to satisfy the tax delinquencies.

IRS' first priority is to secure full payment, which could include short-term payment arrangements not to exceed 60 days. If full payment cannot be secured in the short term and the dollar amount of the delinquency exceeds a certain dollar threshold, Collection employees are required to obtain, from the taxpayer, information about the taxpayer's assets, liabilities, income, and expenses. This information may be collected using IRS' "Collection Information Statement" form.

IRS sometimes collects delinquencies as a result of the refund offset program or annual reminder notices sent to taxpayers who owe smaller amounts. Under the refund offset program, IRS applies any refunds otherwise due the taxpayer to the tax delinquency.

Process for Classifying Delinquencies as CNC

At any stage of the collection process, IRS may determine that collection is not currently possible. At that time the case is closed from active inventory and placed in CNC status. Most CNC classifications occur in the last two stages of the collection process. During the period covered by our review, IRS procedures required filing a notice of lien[5] against a taxpayer's property before an account was classified as CNC if the delinquency exceeded $2,000 (or $500 if the taxpayer had real property).

IRS can classify accounts as CNC for a variety of reasons. The most common reasons for individual taxpayers are that (1) the taxpayer is unable to pay the delinquent tax;[6] (2) IRS is unable to locate the taxpayer or the taxpayer's assets; or (3) IRS is unable to contact the taxpayer, although it has a current address, and is unable to locate any of the taxpayer's assets.

[5]A lien is a claim on the proceeds from any sale of the delinquent taxpayer's property up to the amount of the tax debt. In February 1993, IRS revised the lien filing requirement by increasing the dollar level to all CNC accounts with delinquent assessments greater than $5,000.

[6]The inability to pay reason includes instances when the delinquent taxpayer does not have the resources to pay as well as when the taxpayer has resources but collection of the tax would cause the taxpayer undue financial hardship.

Collection employees use the financial information obtained from the taxpayer, the taxpayer's current tax return, and third parties, such as employers and financial institutions, to determine the taxpayer's ability to pay the taxes owed. IRS requires that the information used be documented and verified, and Collection employees are required to look for any unreported assets. They are also required to analyze asset information to determine the potential for the taxpayer to pay the delinquency from the proceeds of loans secured by equity in the assets or voluntary liquidation or the potential for IRS to collect the taxes owed by seizing and selling the assets. Collection employees are required to use income and expense information to determine the amount of monthly installment payments that the taxpayer can pay if full payment is not possible.

If the Collection employee determines that the taxpayer has insufficient assets to pay the delinquency without causing undue financial hardship, and the taxpayer's monthly necessary living expenses equal or exceed monthly income,[7] the account can be classified as CNC. In analyzing monthly income and expenses, IRS guidance states that only expenses that are necessary and reasonable for the taxpayer's production of income or provide for the health and welfare of the taxpayer and the taxpayer's family should be included.

Generally, before accounts can be classified CNC on the basis of an inability to locate the taxpayer, IRS employees are required to review the latest tax return, analyze asset information, establish that there is no valid telephone number for the taxpayer, query employment bureaus, file liens, and, under certain circumstances, review examination assessments. In addition, IRS employees are required to visit the taxpayer's last known address and contact neighbors to determine the taxpayer's whereabouts. Further, IRS employees are required to get confirmation from the U.S. Postal Service that there is no known address for the taxpayer and to check other sources, such as the local automobile and driver licensing office.

For unable to contact cases, IRS employees are generally required to follow all the procedures required for unable to locate cases, except contact the U.S. Postal Service. They are also required to attempt a telephone contact. Collection employees determine the extent of other investigative work on the basis of their judgment as to the likelihood of collection.

[7] IRS policy states that an installment agreement should be set up when the taxpayer can make regular payments of at least $25 per month (that is, the taxpayer's monthly necessary living expenses are at least $25 less than the taxpayer's monthly income).

Reactivating CNC Accounts

Because the situation for which the account was classified CNC could change—making the account potentially collectible—IRS has set up mechanisms to reactivate these accounts. Although some manual follow-ups can be required, IRS relies heavily on its computer system to monitor new information to determine changes in taxpayers' situations.

For unable to pay CNC accounts, Collection employees use the necessary and reasonable living expense information obtained from the taxpayer to determine the annual income level above which the taxpayer could start making payments. A closing code corresponding to this income level is entered into the computer, and subsequent returns are monitored.[8] Closing codes correspond to annual incomes ranging from $6,000 to $30,000. If a tax return is filed showing income over the level selected, the account will be reactivated and put back into active inventory. However, IRS has established a hold period of 65 weeks during which returns are not monitored for reactivation purposes.

For determining whether unable to locate cases should be reactivated, the computer searches for any subsequently filed tax return or change of address. For unable to contact cases, the computer monitors tax returns filed after the 65-week hold period to determine whether the taxpayer has income greater than $14,000, the level required to reactivate the account. IRS officials were uncertain about why there is a 65-week hold period before reactivation is possible, and they could not explain why the income threshold for reactivation is set at $14,000 for unable to contact cases. Unable to locate and unable to contact accounts will also reactivate if IRS matches the taxpayer with information sources that show the taxpayer has assets, such as bank accounts or wages, that can be levied.

When CNC accounts are reactivated from computer searches, they reenter the collection process at the first stage, the notice process. Unable to locate and contact taxpayers reactivated for the purpose of levying the taxpayers' assets receive only the final notice of intent to levy, while other taxpayers receive all the standard notices. The case then follows the normal collection process through the next two stages. In fiscal year 1992, IRS reactivated accounts with delinquent tax liabilities totaling $1.7 billion.

In addition to the use of automated computer searches of IRS information to reactivate an account, Collection employees may establish a specific mandatory follow-up date when IRS should reexamine a taxpayer's account

[8]IRS does not determine whether these taxpayers use their income for the necessary living expenses they have identified. However, IRS policy does state that they are not allowed to incur additional debt.

to determine if collection is possible. Mandatory follow-up is used when the Collection employee knows of future changes in the taxpayer's situation that would affect the taxpayer's ability to pay but would not be identified through computer searches of IRS information. At district offices we visited, IRS officials told us that the mandatory follow-up cases are kept in tickler files that are monitored by Collection's special procedures function.

IRS Oversight of the CNC Process

IRS' oversight of the CNC process focuses on the initial determination. The primary oversight mechanisms are supervisory review and approval of the initial CNC determination and CNC postreviews, which examine a sample of CNC accounts. Additional oversight is accomplished through the more general Collection Quality Measurement System (CQMS), which reviews samples from all case closures. In addition, IRS has conducted a detailed study of CNC accounts, Currently Not Collectible Study Group Report, dated February 1991, as part of its increased efforts to manage the growing accounts receivable inventory. According to IRS officials, IRS has no systems in place to evaluate its reactivation process and has not done a detailed study to determine whether the reactivation process is operating as intended.

IRS Collection group managers are responsible for approving CNC determinations. Revenue officers use Form 53 (see app. II for a copy of Form 53) to initiate closure of the account as CNC. The form includes a checklist of critical items that may be required, depending on the specific reason for the CNC determination, before the closure is approved. A group manager uses the Form 53 and related case information to determine whether the CNC determination is appropriate and can require the Collection employee to do additional work if necessary. If the group manager agrees with the Collection employee's decision, the group manager will sign the form, and the determination will then be entered into the computer.

The two additional reviews—postreviews and the CQMS reviews—of CNC determinations are done by examining statistical samples of closed accounts. Under the CNC postreview, all accounts with delinquencies over $100,000 and a sample of other CNC accounts are selected for review quarterly.[9] IRS guidance provides instructions and tables for computing required sample sizes. The process for reviewing cases is not standardized, and, within a region, postreviews can either be done by each individual

[9]Prior to January 1, 1990, IRS required review of all accounts with delinquencies greater than $50,000.

district office or all cases in the region can be reviewed at one IRS location within the region. IRS requires that quarterly reports on the results of these reviews be prepared and submitted to the regional offices. Under CQMS, regional office employees review a nonstratified, statistically valid sample of all types of case closures, ranging from full-paid to CNC. These reviews of cases follow a standard process, and each case review is documented on a standard checksheet. These checksheets are compiled and then analyzed by both the regional and national offices.

IRS' detailed CNC study was initiated to identify causes for the increase in the number of accounts and dollars reported as CNC over several years. The study identified the substantial period of time that elapses during IRS' three-stage collection process and internal procedures pertaining to certain types of assessments as the two primary causes of the growth. IRS has increased its use of offers in compromise and installment payments as a means of dealing with CNC cases. IRS' study, however, did not look at specific cases and, thus, did not address the types of issues covered in our report.

CNC Growth Exceeds Collections, and Individual CNC Account Growth Exceeds Business CNC Account Growth

The dollar amount of CNC accounts has been increasing faster than the collection of delinquent taxes. The assessed dollar amount of accounts classified as CNC exceeded the dollars collected by IRS' district office employees in fiscal year 1990 through 1992. Figure 1.2 shows dollars collected and dollars classified as CNC from 1987 through 1992.

Figure 1.2: District Office Collections Compared to Assessed Dollars Added to Currently Not Collectible Status, Fiscal Years 1987 to 1992

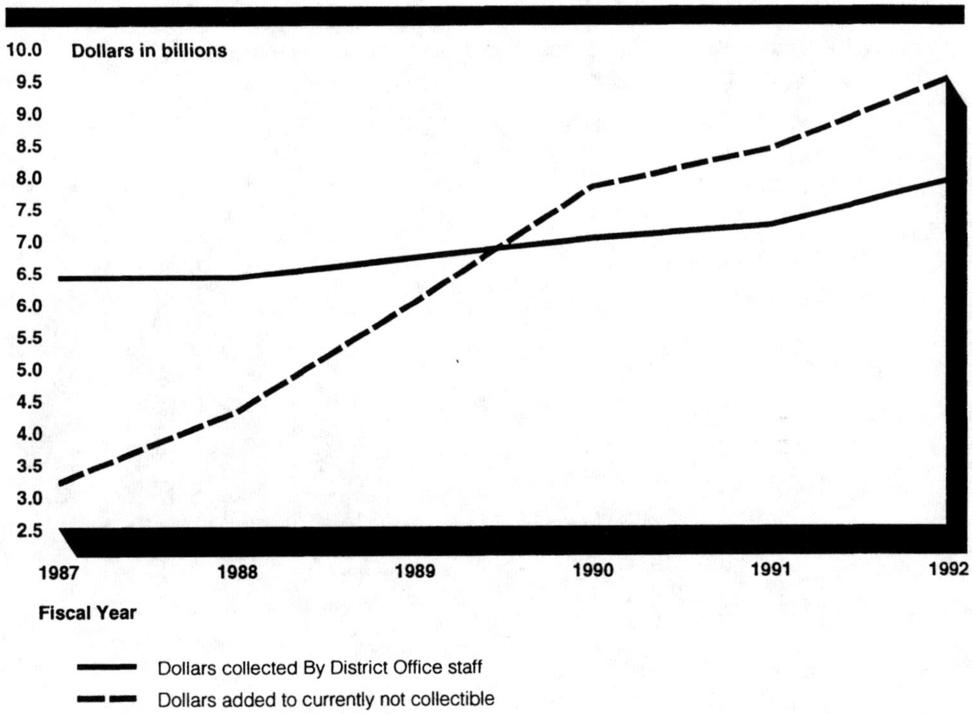

Source: IRS data.

The assessed dollar amounts in the inventory of CNC accounts has grown over 178 percent since 1987, with individual CNC dollar amounts growing faster than business CNC dollar amounts. Figure 1.3 shows the assessed dollar amounts in individual and business CNC accounts at the end of fiscal year 1987 through 1992.

Figure 1.3: CNC Assessed Amounts Posted by Master File, End of Fiscal Years 1987 to 1992

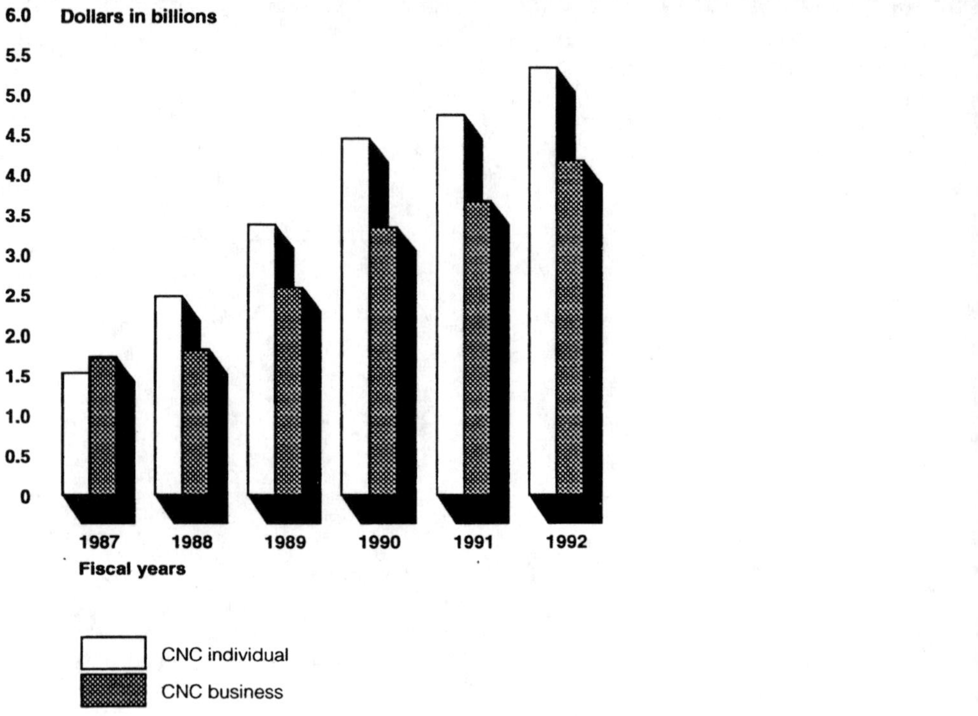

Source: IRS data.

Objectives, Scope, and Methodology

The objectives of this assignment were to determine whether individual taxpayer CNC accounts are properly classified and whether IRS' efforts to monitor these accounts for future collection potential are adequate. To accomplish these objectives, we did the following:

(a) We reviewed the case files of a stratified random sample of 107 individual taxpayer accounts that were classified CNC because of the taxpayer's inability to pay or because IRS was unable to locate or contact the taxpayer during August and September 1991 in 5 IRS district offices.

(b)We reviewed the case files of two judgmentally selected individual taxpayer CNC accounts with delinquencies over $100,000 that were classified CNC during August and September 1991 at one district office.

(c)We reviewed all available IRS CNC postreview reports for fiscal year 1990.

(d)We obtained and analyzed IRS' national database of CNC accounts from IRS' 10 service centers—June 1991 information was obtained from 9 service centers and June 1990 information was obtained from the 10th service center.[10]

(e)We selected a random sample of 100 individual taxpayer CNC accounts classified as unable to pay from the national database as of June 1991 and analyzed the 1990 tax returns of the 52 taxpayers who had filed.

(f)We interviewed IRS national, regional, and district office Collection officials to determine procedures and criteria for classifying accounts as CNC, reviewing and approving CNC determinations, and for reactivating CNC accounts.

To determine whether CNC accounts are properly classified, we reviewed CNC case files from IRS' Albany, Brooklyn, Chicago, Greensboro, and San Jose district offices (items a and b above). We selected these district offices because they provided a mix of geographic locations, workload sizes, CNC disposition rates, and postreview locations. For each office, we had IRS hold all cases classified CNC during August and September 1991 and randomly selected 20 to 30 individual taxpayers who had accounts classified as unable to pay, unable to locate, or unable to contact. We also judgmentally selected two individual taxpayer accounts with delinquencies over $100,000 from one district office to see if large dollar accounts were handled differently. Appendix I describes our sampling and analysis methodology.

In addition, we reviewed all available fiscal year 1990 quarterly CNC postreview reports—the last completed fiscal year at the time of our review—for IRS' 63 district offices and interviewed reviewers and supervisors from 5 district offices to obtain information on the quality of CNC casework (items c and f above). Because the reports did not have a standard format and district offices reported on the prevalence and severity of problems differently, we recorded only whether or not the district office had identified a situation as a problem. In addition, when we had information from district offices on the number of cases that postreviewers had returned to revenue officers each quarter for rework, we calculated the percentage of reviewed cases that had been returned.

[10]The Andover Service Center provided us with the June 1990 database instead of the June 1991 database. By the time the mistake was detected, IRS had destroyed part of the June 1991 information. We included the Andover information in our analyses when timing was not a factor and deleted it when timing would affect the results. Information used in this report is footnoted to indicate when the Andover information is included.

To determine whether IRS' efforts to monitor CNC accounts for future collection potential are adequate, we (1) reviewed the financial information on the 60 unable to pay cases in the 107 district office cases selected for review (item a above); (2) randomly selected 100 taxpayers from IRS' June 1991 national database of CNC accounts and did detailed analyses of the taxpayers' 1990 tax returns (items d and e above); and (3) evaluated IRS' reactivation procedures (items a, e, and f above).

We tested the accuracy of IRS' computerized CNC account information by comparing it with summary information developed from other IRS computerized sources and with information in our sample cases. We found no evidence that the computer information was inaccurate. However, we did not do an independent reliability assessment.

We did our audit work between April 1991 and December 1992 using generally accepted government auditing standards. IRS provided written comments on a draft of this report. These comments are presented and evaluated in chapters 2, 3, and 4 and are reprinted in their entirety in appendix III.

Chapter 2

IRS' Determinations to Classify Accounts as CNC Are Often Inadequate or Questionable

IRS' determinations to classify accounts as CNC and thereby suspend collection action are not always complete or correct and do not always fully provide for future collection potential. Our review of CNC determinations in 5 IRS district offices identified inadequate or questionable actions in an estimated 55 percent of the 1,233 accounts these offices classified as CNC in August and September 1991.[1] According to IRS' records, these accounts contained an estimated $30.7 million in delinquent taxes at the time they were classified as CNC. This situation has allowed some taxpayers who reported 1990 incomes of more than $70,000 and who continued to earn significant income when their accounts were classified as CNC to pay nothing towards their delinquent tax debts. Our review also showed that in an estimated 22 percent of the unable to pay CNC cases, IRS failed to file liens or otherwise appropriately provide for future collection potential.

These problems are not new. We reported similar problems in November 1981,[2] and IRS' internal audit and Collection studies and reviews have also reported such problems. The problems appear to be caused by the lack of specific criteria to make the CNC determinations and the insufficient actions to prevent inappropriate CNC determinations.

IRS Guidance for CNC Determinations

If IRS employees determine during the collection process that collection is not currently possible or would cause substantial hardship to the taxpayer, the account is to be classified as CNC. According to IRS policy, if collection of the delinquency would prevent the taxpayer from meeting necessary and reasonable living expenses, the taxpayer's account may be classified as CNC because of the taxpayer's inability to pay. The Collection employee is required to examine the taxpayer's assets, liabilities, income, and expenses before classifying an account as CNC. This is to be done through independent record checks as well as thorough analysis of information provided by the taxpayer.

IRS policy allows its employees to classify accounts as CNC on the basis of inability to pay regardless of the amount of the taxpayer's income. IRS policy indicates what types of expenses might be reasonable and necessary (food, housing, transportation, etc.), but it does not provide

[1]The problems identified are discussed by category in the remainder of the chapter. The cumulative percentage of the categories exceeds 55 percent because some cases had more than one type of problem. Sampling errors for the estimates developed from our case file review are shown in table I.2 of app. I.

[2]What IRS Can Do To Collect More Delinquent Taxes (GAO/GGD-82-4, Nov. 5, 1981).

guidance on how to determine the dollar amounts or ranges that should be considered reasonable for each of these expenses[3] or the amounts that should be considered reasonable for total living expenses when taxpayer circumstances differ. IRS officials believe that the Collection employees working the cases are in the best position to make these decisions.

During the collection process, IRS requires that Collection employees search internal and external sources for leads to use in locating delinquent taxpayers and their assets. IRS policy states that after reasonable attempts to locate and contact the taxpayer and locate the taxpayer's assets have failed, the account may be classified as CNC. For accounts being actively pursued in the third stage of the collection process, IRS policy specifically requires revenue officers to check third-party records, attempt telephone calls to the taxpayer, and visit the last known address before suspending collection action.

Before a case is closed as CNC, a supervisor must approve the determination. In addition, the determination may be subsequently reviewed through the IRS postreview program to determine whether the case was worked correctly. These oversight measures are designed to correct problems as they are identified as well as influence the future behavior of IRS employees through direct feedback and through making procedural changes in how cases are worked (see ch. 4).

Inadequate or Questionable IRS Actions in Some CNC Determinations

Inadequate reviews of taxpayers' financial status, including unquestioned acceptance of what taxpayers' consider necessary and reasonable living expenses, computations that exclude some income, and inadequate asset checks, have resulted in Collection employees suspending collection actions on taxpayers' accounts without substantiating the inability to pay. In addition, employees' failure to follow asset and address leads has caused them to suspend collection actions before making reasonable efforts to locate or contact the taxpayers.

A significant problem we found in IRS' determinations of taxpayers' ability to pay was IRS' allowance of what appeared to be expenses that exceeded necessary and reasonable living expenses. In determining necessary and reasonable living expenses, we questioned payments for such necessities as housing, transportation, and utilities if they appeared high in relation to the location and family circumstances. In our opinion, taxpayers should

[3]IRS procedures allow payments for other debt, such as credit card debt, but require that they be limited to minimum required payments.

not be able to avoid payment of taxes by living beyond their means, and taxpayers should not be able to finance such expenses with money that is owed in back federal taxes. This type of situation is unfair to all those taxpayers who live within their means and pay their taxes. We estimate that 12 percent of unable to pay cases were of this type. These were cases in which IRS allowed large mortgage payments and leases for expensive cars as necessary and reasonable living expenses. Some examples of the problem cases follow:

- Married taxpayers with no dependents earned nearly $80,000 a year and owed $123,000 in back taxes. Their financial statement showed expenses that exceeded income by almost $275 a month. IRS allowed as necessary living expenses monthly life insurance payments of $450 and over $900 in monthly payments on debts to credit card companies and other creditors.[4]
- A taxpayer was earning $28,000 a year and owed $14,000 in back taxes. The taxpayer claimed a $120 monthly telephone expense, which IRS allowed as a reasonable and necessary living expense.
- Married taxpayers with four dependents were earning almost $80,000 a year and owed $75,000 in taxes for 1984 through 1990. IRS allowed a monthly mortgage expense of $1,800 and payments for two cars totaling about $950 per month as necessary living expenses.

We also found a number of cases in which taxpayers' reported expenses exceeded reported income by several hundred dollars a month with no explanation of the source of the funds used to pay the excess expenses. In one such case, a self-employed single taxpayer claimed living expenses that exceeded income by $670 a month, yet no explanation was provided in the case file regarding this difference.

We also found some cases in which IRS did not properly calculate the taxpayer's income.

- A divorced taxpayer owing $25,000 in taxes reported biweekly income of $566—which IRS doubled to calculate a monthly amount. Using this computation, the taxpayer's monthly income and expenses were equal. Had income been calculated correctly, accounting for the fact that in 2 months of the year the taxpayer would receive three paychecks, the taxpayer would have had an excess of $67 a month to pay toward the tax delinquency.

[4]This particular case was not part of the statistical sample but was judgmentally selected as one of the two large-dollar individual taxpayer CNC accounts that were classified as CNC during August and September 1991 at one district office.

We also found that IRS did not make appropriate record checks to identify assets or did not adequately determine the amount of equity available for collection in an estimated 13 percent of the unable to pay CNC cases in the districts we reviewed.

- Married taxpayers owed IRS $75,000 for 1984-1990 income taxes. They refinanced their residence in late 1990 and were to use the proceeds to pay off some personal debts. While earlier financial statements indicated the taxpayers had over $50,000 in equity in their residence, the case file did not indicate the amount obtained from the refinancing. Although the case was being actively worked by revenue officers, none of this money was used to pay back taxes, and none of the taxpayers' monthly payments on personal debts decreased in the taxpayers' February 1991 financial statement used to support the CNC determination. In fact, as a result of the mortgage refinancing, the taxpayers' mortgage payment increased from approximately $900 to nearly $1,800 a month, an expense that was included in the 1991 financial statement. The increased mortgage payment resulted in the taxpayers' expenses exceeding income by more than $400 a month, and IRS classified the case as CNC.

Even when IRS determined that the taxpayer could make payments, it still closed one case as CNC.

- A married taxpayer was individually liable for over $130,000 in 1986-1988 income taxes assessed against profits from criminal activities. The revenue officer determined that the taxpayer's current income exceeded current expenses by $115 a month but recorded that the case was closed as CNC instead of establishing an installment agreement, because the monthly payments would not cover the interest accruing on the liability.

In unable to locate and unable to contact cases, assets can serve as both a source of potential collection and as leads to locate or contact a taxpayer. IRS sometimes failed to follow up on such leads. In one case, the file contained information on a number of banks where at one time the taxpayer had accounts. However, these banks were not contacted by the revenue officer to locate the taxpayer.

IRS also failed to always take the required and prudent steps to locate taxpayers.

- A taxpayer owed $31,000 for 1987. IRS closed the case as an unable to locate CNC without obtaining confirmation that the U.S. Postal Service had no known address for the taxpayer or visiting an address obtained from a credit bureau report.

Future Collection Potential Not Always Protected

When classifying an account CNC, IRS can provide for the possibility of future collection through filing a federal tax lien, selecting the appropriate closing code, or requiring mandatory follow-up. In our review of CNC cases, we found that future collection potential was not protected in an estimated 22 percent of all unable to pay cases. We found cases in which liens were not filed and cases in which IRS set inappropriate closing codes. We did not find any cases that should have been designated for mandatory follow-up.

Liens were required to be filed in an estimated 90 percent of the 1,233 CNC cases from the 5 districts. Although required liens were filed in all but a few cases, we estimate that in 38 percent of the cases the files did not contain copies of lien filing notices as required. Without examining lien filing notices, supervisors could not be sure that the information on the filed liens was accurate and that IRS therefore had priority claims against taxpayers' property.

IRS guidance states that closing codes should be set at an income level that would allow for payments to be made against the tax debt after reasonable and necessary expenses are considered. However, IRS does not provide any specific guidance on how this should be determined. The guidance states only that the Collection employee should consider the level of income necessary to meet basic living expenses, impact of inflation, changes in family size, nontaxable income, and other factors.

We estimate that IRS set the income levels for reactivation at levels greater than were necessary to meet expenses and start paying off the tax liability in 20 percent of unable to pay cases. In determining whether the reactivation income levels were too high, we used the expenses shown by the taxpayer and a 30-percent factor for required withholding from gross pay to determine the income level needed to cover expenses. We then compared that to the income level selected by IRS. We considered any case where IRS set the reactivation level more than two levels higher—$6,000—as being set too high.[5] This can prevent timely

[5]CNC closing codes correspond to income levels that are used to reactivate CNC cases. There are nine closing codes—income levels—at $3,000 intervals between $6,000 and $30,000.

reactivation or prevent reactivation entirely for some accounts that would warrant additional collection effort. We found cases for which there was no apparent relationship between allowed expenses and the closing code selected. For example:

- A taxpayer with no dependents claimed annual expenses of approximately $17,000 and income of approximately $13,000. However, the revenue officer set the closing code at a reactivation income level of $30,000, with no explanation for why this closing code was selected.

In another example, the file did not contain complete financial information.

- A self-employed husband and wife claimed no income and did not distinguish between business and personal living expenses. The only identifiable nonbusiness expense item claimed was $250 a month for food, and the closing code was set at $21,000 without explanation.

IRS' Comments on Our Case Analyses

We discussed all the cases that we identified as having inadequate or questionable actions with IRS district office officials who generally agreed with our findings, but they did not believe that the CNC determination should be changed. Two district offices offered to follow up on the cases and reported that they had taken corrective actions to address some of our concerns, but the CNC classifications had not changed as a result. The corrective actions that district offices took included lowering some closing codes, documenting previously undocumented actions, and pursuing asset and address leads. However, IRS district office officials were unwilling to reevaluate the revenue officers' expense analyses, stating that these were within the revenue officers' judgmental discretion. Because the expense analyses are key to determining collection potential and establishing closing codes, we continue to believe that some of these cases may have collection potential that IRS has not adequately considered.

IRS' Postreviews of CNC Cases Identified Problems

From our review of IRS' CNC postreview reports,[6] we found that more than 40 percent of the district offices reported problems, such as inappropriate closing code selections, sources of information not checked or documented, inadequate reviews of the latest tax return, and cases in which additional collection efforts were warranted. In addition, more than

[6]In chapter 4 of this report, we state several concerns about IRS' CNC postreview program.

20 percent of the district offices reported that mandatory follow-up was not appropriately done and financial analysis of cases was incomplete.

We also found that 20 of 31 district offices reporting data had returned at least 10 percent of the cases they reviewed during fiscal year 1990 to revenue officers. Five district offices returned 20 percent or more of the cases they reviewed. Reasons that postreviewers can return cases to revenue officers include (1) the CNC determination was rejected on the basis of case file information, (2) supporting documents were missing, (3) additional information was required, (4) the reviewer wanted to provide the revenue officer with information related to the casework, and (5) the casework was commendatory. Where the district office identified the reason the case was returned, over 90 percent were returned for additional information. Less than 3 percent were returned because the reviewer wanted to provide information only or because of commendatory work.

One IRS region tracks dollars collected from returned postreview cases. This region's quarterly reports for fiscal year 1990 showed that at least $381,700 should be collected from cases postreviewers returned for rework. The reports also indicated that an additional $296,000 might be collected from future levies.

IRS Does Not Require Payments From Taxpayers Based on the Amount of Their Incomes

IRS does not require payments from taxpayers, regardless of the amount of their income, as long as they have commensurate expenses. We have previously presented examples in which taxpayers who earned more than $70,000 annually had their accounts classified as CNC. (See p. 23.) In addition, our analysis of a database of all individual taxpayers with unable to pay CNC accounts as of July 1991 showed that 8.5 percent of the cases subject to the 65-week reactivation hold reported earning more than $50,000 in 1990.[7]

Although IRS policy allows an account to be classified as CNC when a taxpayer's expenses exceed the taxpayer's net income, it has not set any limits on amount of income a taxpayer can be earning and have an account classified as CNC. However, the highest reactivation level for CNC cases that IRS can set is $30,000. Some IRS officials have expressed reservations about closing accounts as CNC when taxpayers have incomes over the highest reactivation level. National office officials stated that any case in which a delinquent taxpayer earns more than $30,000 a year should be strongly considered for an installment agreement. In addition, the Assistant

[7]See chapter 3 for more information regarding the 65-week reactivation hold.

Regional Commissioner for Collections in one region has distributed guidelines that state that "normally" taxpayers with current incomes in excess of $30,000 per year should have the ability to make some payment on delinquent taxes, barring an unusual circumstance such as severe illness.

Conclusions

Our review and IRS' CNC postreviews indicate that delinquent tax cases are often classified as CNC on the basis of work that is inadequate or questionable or that does not provide for future collection potential. IRS' lack of specific criteria, particularly for determining allowable expenses and for setting the case closing codes, contribute to this problem. In addition, better documentation of IRS' actions as well as additional verification of taxpayers' expense claims could improve CNC determinations. Better supervisory reviews and better use of postreviews, which are addressed further in chapter 4 of this report, provide additional ways to improve the quality of CNC determinations.

Our work also revealed that IRS does not always require payments from taxpayers who earn higher than average incomes if they claim commensurate expenses. We share the concern of some IRS officials that accounts for taxpayers with incomes above some level should not be classified as CNC unless there are extraordinary circumstances. Further, we believe IRS should require at least minimum payments from delinquent taxpayers who have high incomes.[8] The benefits of such a requirement would be numerous. It would remind taxpayers of their tax debts and IRS' seriousness about collecting them. It would provide a basic sense of fairness, since other taxpayers are required to pay when they earn much less.[9] Most importantly, it would result in the collection of additional dollars due the U.S. Treasury.

Recommendations

We recommend that the Commissioner of Internal Revenue

- establish specific guidelines for determining taxpayers' ability to pay delinquent taxes, including criteria for determining dollar ranges for reasonable and necessary expenses;

[8] We also found unable to pay CNC accounts for self-employed persons reporting in excess of $100,000 gross receipts who could similarly be required to make at least minimum payments to IRS.

[9] We found cases where IRS determined that taxpayers who had annual incomes ranging from $6,000 to $30,000 had the ability to make payments on their tax debts.

- establish specific guidelines for selecting the income level at which unable to pay CNC accounts will be reactivated; and
- require, except in extraordinary situations, at least minimum payments from delinquent taxpayers with incomes above a specified level.

Agency Comments and Our Evaluation

In an August 5, 1993, letter commenting on a draft of this report, the Commissioner of Internal Revenue agreed that IRS needs better guidelines for determining taxpayer ability to pay delinquent taxes, including criteria for determining dollar ranges for reasonable and necessary expenses. Toward that end, IRS plans to contact federal agencies responsible for management and collection of federal debt to determine how they approach similar situations in order to develop a framework for general guidelines. The Commissioner stated that because these actions are a substantial departure from IRS' usual method of operations, the involvement of Collection executives and top-level management is essential to ensure these changes are accepted in IRS' front-line operations. According to the Commissioner, these actions are a long-term commitment to improving the quality of CNC determinations.

The Commissioner agreed with our recommendation to establish specific guidelines for selecting an income level at which unable to pay CNC accounts will be reactivated and agreed to include specific language in the next revision of relevant portions of the Internal Revenue Manual (IRM).

The Commissioner agreed in principle that IRS should require, except in extraordinary situations, minimum payments from delinquent taxpayers with incomes above a specified level. However, rather than set an income level, the Commissioner preferred to emphasize through additional IRM guidelines that the determination of the hardship conditions should not include items that are lifestyle choices, especially where such choices limit the ability of the taxpayers to pay their tax debts. The Commissioner stated that the disallowance of personal choice items is an issue that will vary on a case-by-case basis. We agree that additional IRM guidelines may assist IRS employees in making hardship determinations. However, while exceptions might occur on the basis of individual situations, we also believe that IRS employees would be better assisted in making such determinations if specific income level guidelines requiring minimum payments were used.

Chapter 3

CNC Monitoring and Reactivation Processes Need to Be Strengthened

IRS is losing the potential of collecting delinquent tax debts because of its inefficient processes for monitoring and reactivating CNC accounts. Our analysis showed that cases with collection potential were not being identified and reactivated because IRS

- places an arbitrary 65-week reactivation hold on accounts classified as CNC because of taxpayers' inability to pay;
- tracks only one taxpayer, rather than both taxpayers with a joint delinquency, when the taxpayers become divorced, separated, or otherwise file separate tax returns; and
- considers only income in determining when to reactivate unable to pay and unable to contact CNC accounts, rather than the full array of collection potential indicators available from tax returns and information returns.

In addition, once most CNC accounts are reactivated, IRS delays, and possibly loses, collections because of its inefficient collection practices for reactivated accounts.

IRS' 65-Week Hold Period Results in Undue Reactivation Delays in Some Cases

On the basis of our analysis of over 300,000 individual taxpayer accounts classified as CNC as of July 1991, we estimate that almost 36,000[1] of the unable to pay accounts, or 11 percent, totaling about $250 million in delinquencies would have been reactivated on the basis of returns filed in 1991 had the 65-week hold period not prevented reactivation. These returns showed income that exceeded the reactivation levels established by IRS when the cases were classified as CNC. Under current reactivation procedures, these 36,000 accounts will remain in CNC status until future income tax returns show income that exceeds reactivation income levels, the tax debts are paid voluntarily or as a result of IRS' offsetting any refunds due the taxpayers, or the collection statute of limitations expires.

Further analysis of these 36,000 accounts showed that the taxpayers reported income that averaged $10,000 more than the income needed for reactivation. The amount of income over the reactivation level ranged from $1 to $92,000. Forty-three percent of the taxpayers reported income of more than $30,000, and 8.5 percent reported income over $50,000. While our analysis indicated the existence of collection potential, we did not have information on taxpayers' expenses and therefore do not know whether collections were actually possible.

[1]These 36,000 individual taxpayer accounts, from the 9 service centers that provided us with 1991 information were classified as CNC between January 15, 1990, and June 30, 1991.

IRS officials could not tell us why the 65-week hold period was adopted. They noted, however, that it allows a complete tax year to elapse before reactivation is possible and that without it, some cases would be reactivated within months of their CNC determination, when taxpayers' circumstances would probably not have changed. This could happen if a case was classified as CNC after the end of the year but before the tax return was filed.

While the 65-week hold period does prevent unnecessary reactivation in some cases, it also prevents pursuing timely collection in others. The hold period could prevent an account from being reactivated for almost 2 years after it is classified as CNC regardless of changes in the taxpayer's financial situation. For example, an account classified as CNC in February 1990 because of the taxpayer's inability to pay could not be reactivated until May 1991. Even then, the account would not be reactivated until the taxpayer filed a tax return that showed income above the reactivation level. This probably would not occur before January 1992.

IRS Does Not Track Both Taxpayers When Monitoring a Joint CNC Account

On the basis of our review of a sample of the 1,233 accounts classified as CNC in the 5 district offices during August and September 1991, we estimate that 12 percent of the accounts involved a joint delinquency and taxpayers who were separated, divorced, or filing separately at the time their joint accounts were classified as CNC. In such situations, IRS attempts collection from both spouses, but it determines a closing code for only one of them. Thus, for tracking and reactivation purposes, IRS ignores future collection potential from the other spouse.[2] IRS cannot link both spouses to the delinquent account and thereby track both spouses, because its computer system can use only one Social Security number to identify a joint individual taxpayer account.[3]

In unable to pay cases involving joint delinquencies and taxpayers that are still filing jointly at the time the account is classified CNC, IRS selects a reactivation code on the basis of the combined income that would be needed for the couple to meet their necessary and reasonable combined living expenses. If the taxpayers subsequently separate, divorce, or file separate returns, not only will IRS ignore the income of the secondary

[2]However, IRS can use the future refunds of either spouse to offset the joint delinquency.

[3]IRS uses the Social Security number of the taxpayer whose name appears first on the tax return to identify a joint account. This person is referred to as the primary spouse. The primary spouse designation in no way indicates which spouse has the greater income or potential for paying the delinquent tax debt.

spouse for reactivation purposes, it will continue to use the reactivation income for the primary spouse that is based on the former couple's combined living expenses rather than on the primary spouse's individual living expenses. Thus, the account may not reactivate when either or both of the taxpayers could make payments.

The following are examples of situations we found in our sample:

- Separated taxpayers were jointly liable for 1987 income tax. IRS determined that both taxpayers were unable to pay and selected a reactivation level of $24,000 to use in tracking the primary spouse's income. The secondary spouse's income was not tracked.
- Separated taxpayers were jointly liable for $21,000 in taxes for 1983-1987. IRS located the secondary spouse and found that she did not have the ability to pay the delinquent taxes. Her monthly expenses exceeded her income by $33. IRS could not find the primary spouse and classified the joint account as an unable to locate CNC account. Because the account was classified as CNC on the basis of IRS not being able to locate the primary spouse and because IRS ignores the income of the secondary spouse, IRS will not reactivate the account on the basis of the secondary spouse's income even if her income increases substantially.

IRS officials told us that they are currently trying to determine whether they can enhance their ability to monitor joint CNC accounts with their current computer system. They also said that they would consider the use of primary and secondary Social Security numbers as part of Tax Systems Modernization, IRS' multiyear, multibillion-dollar redesign of its automated systems.

IRS' Reactivation Criteria Do Not Consider All Indicators of Collection Potential

IRS reactivates unable to pay and unable to contact CNC accounts on the basis of income computed from information on taxpayers' tax returns. However, tax returns contain other indicators of collection potential that IRS does not use as reactivation criteria.

From our review of the 1990 tax returns of a random sample of individual taxpayers who had unable to pay CNC accounts as of July 1991, we identified four returns that contained indicators of collection potential that

IRS did not use.[4] In three cases, the taxpayers each reported interest income of more than $400. Assuming an interest rate of 4 percent, compounded annually for the year 1990, reported interest of $400 would indicate $10,000 in interest-bearing assets. In another case, the taxpayer reported almost $760 in dividend income, as well as proceeds of more than $33,000 from the sale of long-term assets. Like interest income, dividend income indicates the existence of underlying assets. These assets, as well as proceeds from the sale of assets, could be used as sources of funds for the payment of tax debts when taxpayers' incomes are less than the reactivation income levels. If IRS had reactivation criteria that included all indicators of collection potential, more delinquent tax debts might be collected through levies, seizures, or taxpayer cooperation.

IRS' Collection Practices for Most Reactivated Accounts Are Inefficient

When CNC accounts are reactivated, they are placed in the active accounts receivable inventory. Unless the taxpayers initiate actions to resolve their accounts, most reactivated accounts go back to the first notice and proceed through the three-stage collection process as if they were newly assessed delinquencies.[5] Although the taxpayers already know they owe tax debts from prior communications, IRS sends out the entire series of notices over a 6-month period before attempting to make personal contact. Also, even though IRS has already worked these accounts and determined that the taxpayers now have the ability to pay, these accounts are not given higher priority than unworked accounts.

Generally, employees who work reactivated accounts do not have the information that was in the prior case files. According to IRS officials, prior case files are not readily available and are seldom obtained. The prior case file contains the case history, including information that would allow employees working the reactivated case to identify changes in the taxpayer's situation since the case was classified as CNC.

Conclusions

IRS may have missed opportunities to collect delinquent tax debts because accounts with collection potential have remained in CNC status and therefore have not been pursued. In addition, even when CNC accounts are

[4]We reviewed a random sample of 100 individual taxpayers from IRS' national database of CNC accounts (including Andover service center accounts). At the time of our review, only 52 of the taxpayers in our sample had filed 1990 tax returns. The number of returns that contained indicators of collection potential was not large enough to provide meaningful statistical estimates for the population of unable to pay CNC taxpayers.

[5]If an unable to contact or unable to locate CNC account is reactivated because a new levy source has been identified, IRS sends the taxpayer only the final notice of intent to levy.

reactivated, IRS does not take advantage of information about the accounts that could facilitate collections.

The 65-week reactivation hold period prevents timely collection action when the situation that led to the CNC classification changes. In addition, IRS' practices with regard to the tracking of taxpayers with joint delinquencies when they separate, divorce, or file separate tax returns have resulted in the potential of collecting from one, and in some instances, both, taxpayers being ignored. Further, as a result of using income as the sole indicator of collection potential, IRS has overlooked other potential sources of funds for the payment of delinquent tax debts. Finally, more expeditious handling of reactivated accounts and increased use of information about the account prior to its classification as CNC could result in more collections.

Recommendations

We recommend that the Commissioner of Internal Revenue

- eliminate the automatic 65-week reactivation hold period and allow employees to determine when each CNC account should be considered for reactivation purposes;
- track both taxpayers with joint delinquencies to ensure that each taxpayer's ability to pay or status is considered in the reactivation decision;
- study the benefits of using other pertinent information, such as interest and dividend income and proceeds from the sale of assets, in addition to total income as reactivation criteria; and
- expedite the processing of reactivated cases by reducing the number of notices and making prior case files readily available for IRS employees working reactivated cases.

Agency Comments and Our Evaluation

The Commissioner did not agree with our recommendation to eliminate the automatic 65-week reactivation hold period and allow employees to determine when CNC accounts should be considered for reactivation. The Commissioner commented that the 65-week hold exists for sound administrative reasons in that it prevents reactivation of a case on the basis of income that has already been considered. As we pointed out in the report, the hold does prevent unnecessary reactivation in some cases; however, it also prevents timely collections in others. In our sample, almost a quarter of the taxpayers were classified CNC during the first 6 months of 1990 filed 1990 tax returns with incomes exceeding their reactivation level. Because of the 65-week hold, these cases would not even have been considered for reactivation until the taxpayers filed their 1991 tax returns sometime in 1992. We believe that some revision to the 65-week hold is needed to ensure the timely reactivation of cases based on tax returns filed within the hold period because income on those returns was not fully considered or known at the time the case was classified as CNC.

We do not believe that mandatory follow-up as proposed by the Commissioner is a substitute for revising the 65-week hold. First, mandatory follow-up is currently available but not used in the situations we identified. Second, mandatory follow-up would require the manual review of individual case files and tax returns, which would be done more efficiently by computer.

The Commissioner agreed in principle with the remaining recommendations to track both taxpayers with joint liabilities, use all pertinent available indicators of collection as reactivation criteria, and expedite the processing of reactivated cases and make prior information available to IRS employees.

The Commissioner commented that the current system does not have the ability to track the collection of two taxpayers for a joint liability and that this issue, as noted in the report, would be pursued as an element of Tax Systems Modernization. Because the modernization efforts are long-term, it is not clear when IRS will take the actions needed to correct this problem. Since IRS systems currently check both taxpayers for potential refund offsets, we believe IRS should consider what actions could be taken in the short term to track both taxpayers' income in joint delinquency cases.

Regarding the use of other available information as criteria for reactivating CNC cases, the Commissioner believes the problem may lie with the CNC investigations and should be resolved with better investigations. We agree that some of the problem could be resolved with better investigations. However, all this information may not be available at the time of the investigation. Our sample was taken from the universe of CNC accounts and not just ones recently classified CNC. Although our sample was small, we found instances where IRS could have used other tax return information as indicators of collection potential. Although we were not able to measure the extent of its value, we continue to believe there is potential for using this information in addition to income as indicators of collection potential. Therefore, our revised recommendation is that IRS further study the benefits of using such information.

Although the Commissioner stated that there may be benefits to reducing the number of notices sent to delinquent taxpayers and providing prior case file information to employees working reactivated cases, she did not say that IRS intends to change its procedures. We continue to believe that IRS needs to change its procedures to ensure that reactivated cases are sent fewer notices and that employees are provided with the prior case file information at the time the account is reactivated. According to the Commissioner, prior case files are available from the Federal Records Center and should be requested as needed. We did not find any situation where the prior case files were obtained and reviewed in our sample cases. IRS region and district officials said during the review that it would be difficult, if not impossible, to locate CNC case files once they were shipped to the Federal Records Center because there was no inventory of specific cases.

Chapter 4

IRS' Oversight Is Not Effective in Identifying and Correcting Inappropriate CNC Determinations

IRS' annual assessment of the Collection function's progress in accomplishing its strategic goals, internal audit efforts, special studies, and CQMS, CNC post-, and supervisory reviews are all oversight mechanisms that could identify problems in IRS' CNC determination process. However, the primary oversight mechanisms are the supervisory and CNC postreviews. Supervisory approval is required before an account can be classified as CNC, and postreviews focus on a sample of accounts that have already been classified as CNC. Our analysis of supervisory and CNC postreviews identified limitations in their scope and reporting practices that may allow the inadequate and questionable actions we identified to continue. In addition, we noted some positive steps IRS has taken that could decrease the number of CNC accounts.

Supervisory Reviews Do Not Prevent Inappropriate CNC Determinations

As a result of our review of CNC determinations in 5 district offices, we believe that IRS supervisors should not have approved an estimated 55 percent of the 1,233 accounts classified as CNC in August and September 1991. (See ch. 2 for a further discussion of the results of our review.) According to Collection supervisors and other IRS officials, in some instances the immediate supervisors may not have sufficient time to fully review CNC determinations, and they rely heavily on the judgment of the Collection employees who made the initial determinations.

Because of the limited guidance on how to determine reasonable and necessary living expenses, Collection employees' judgment plays a significant role in the determination that taxpayers are unable to pay their delinquent tax debts. In commenting on the CNC determinations we identified as inappropriate, IRS district office officials stated that the questionable determinations were within employees' discretion. Although some expenses may seem unreasonable, the IRS officials stated that the employee making the initial determination probably had other information that justified the CNC determination that was not shown in the case file.

Under IRS' current system of evaluating staff performance, accounts classified "currently not collectible" are given the same weight as dollars collected. Other factors, such as the age of cases, case turnover, and case closures are given greater importance as indicators of performance. Thus, Collection employees have little incentive to continue to pursue these accounts and their supervisors have little incentive to question their judgment. Although IRS' appraisal scheme predates it, current tax law prohibits IRS from using collection performance statistics to evaluate, compensate, or reward employees. Congress, long concerned that collection performance might be interpreted as quotas that might induce IRS staff to mistreat taxpayers, added this provision in 1988 to protect taxpayers from such actions. In an earlier report, we suggested that Congress consider revising this provision.[1]

CNC Postreviews Are Not Always Done

As a result of our review of all available fiscal year 1990 CNC postreview reports, we found that almost all district offices did postreviews for each quarterly period. However, the district offices did not always do CNC postreviews of the number of accounts required by IRS policy. Our comparison of the number of CNC accounts that the district offices were required to review with the number they reviewed showed that 35 of 43[2] district offices did less than 75 percent of their required reviews for the fiscal year. This included district offices in the Southwest Region, which did not review any accounts with delinquencies of less than $100,000. Sixteen of the district offices not in the Southwest Region reviewed less than 50 percent of the number of CNC accounts required. These shortfalls sometimes meant that several hundred CNC accounts that should have been reviewed were not.

IRS national office officials told us that they do not know whether district offices are in current compliance with the postreview selection requirements. However, they said that since fiscal year 1990, there has been increased IRS-wide emphasis on CNC accounts and that this increased emphasis may have led to improvements in oversight efforts. National office reports of visits to selected district offices to assess their progress in achieving strategic goals during fiscal year 1992 noted progress in the postreview function in two regions.

IRS officials we talked to at three regional offices said they check CNC postreview account selections to varying degrees. One official told us that she did not determine the number of accounts that should have been selected for review, but she did look at postreview reports to determine whether the number of selected accounts was in the "ballpark."

[1]Tax Administration: New Delinquent Tax Collection Methods for IRS (GAO/GGD-93-67, May 11, 1993).

[2]Only 43 of the 63 district offices provided information that allowed us to determine the number of CNC accounts they were required to review.

Postreviewers Sometimes Overlook Problems

Some of the August and September 1991 CNC accounts we reviewed from two of the five district offices had also been reviewed in the postreview program. We found several inadequate or questionable actions (see ch. 2) that the postreviewers did not identify. An official in one district office attributed this to the fact that the person conducting the postreview was new and that there had been disruptions caused by the district office's transition to a new postreview system. The postreviewer in the other district office wrote in a memorandum to the chief of the Collection division that, except in unusual circumstances, he relied on revenue officers' judgment in determining reasonable and necessary living expenses and appropriate reactivation closing codes.

Postreview Report Formats Are Not Standardized

The postreview reports we obtained varied from a compilation of postreview forms that accompanied returned cases to exhaustive reports that included trend analysis and data on dollars collected from previously returned cases.

Some reports did not provide meaningful information. For example, one district office's report noted that 240 CNC accounts were reviewed for the quarter and that 95 errors were identified during the review. However, the report did not indicate whether a few accounts had several errors or many accounts had a few errors. In addition, the report did not indicate how many of these accounts were returned on the basis of the postreview. The report also did not address trends, even though the error rate had increased over 160 percent from the prior quarter. Information, such as the number of errors per case, number of returned cases, and trends, is needed to determine what, if any, action should be taken.

CNC Postreview Results Are Not Collected and Analyzed to Identify National Systemic Problems

Our September 30, 1991, report, Tax Administration: Opportunities to Increase Revenue Before Expiration of the Statutory Collection Period (GAO/GGD-91-89), stated that IRS' national office does not receive information on the results of CNC postreviews. In that report, we recommended that the Commissioner of Internal Revenue systematically collect and analyze local review results on the decisions to classify accounts as CNC to help identify potential systemic problems that may need correction. IRS agreed with the recommendation; however, as of December 1992, it had not been implemented.

IRS is still identifying various options for capturing and analyzing postreview results. Currently, the national office's only source of nationwide information on CNC determinations is CQMS results, which pertain to CNC and all other types of closed accounts. The CQMS review and reporting format are standardized, and according to IRS officials, the national office uses CQMS results to do trend analyses. IRS officials said that they are considering combining the CQMS and postreview program to address our recommendation.

Some Recent IRS Actions Could Affect the Number of CNC Accounts

IRS has several initiatives underway that could affect the number of CNC accounts. For example, according to IRS officials, initiatives are in place to address almost all the recommendations in IRS' February 1991 CNC study, including reducing the time that current collection procedures require and modifying examination procedures to consider collectibility. IRS has also adopted new policies for allowing taxpayers to (1) settle their tax delinquencies by paying less than their full debts when the amounts paid equal or exceed the amounts IRS could realistically expect to collect through its normal collection process and (2) pay their tax debts in installments over a period of time. Further, IRS officials stated that they plan to develop profile information on taxpayers with CNC accounts. According to IRS officials, the profile information will be more useful in refining its payroll tax delinquency identification and processing than for the CNC accounts discussed in this report.

Conclusions

IRS' two primary CNC determination oversight mechanisms—supervisory and postreviews—have not always been effective in identifying and correcting problems.

The inadequate and questionable actions that we found in our reviews are as much the responsibility of the supervisor as the Collection employees who initiated the actions. Although the Internal Revenue Manual requires supervisory reviews, they have not always been thorough and therefore have not ensured that all required and prudent steps have been taken before accounts have been classified as CNC and collection action thereby suspended.

We believe one reason is the evaluation system in which CNC accounts are given the same weight as dollars collected. In an earlier report, we raised this issue as a matter for congressional consideration. Current tax law would need to be revised for IRS to use collection performance in determining compensation and rewards for its collection staff—a prudent step as long as other criteria, such as fair and courteous treatment of taxpayers, are also considered.

Similar to supervisory reviews, CNC postreview processes have not ensured that the proper number of postreviews are done appropriately, postreview reports provide meaningful information, and postreview results are collected and analyzed so that national systemic problems can be identified.

Improved IRS oversight of the CNC determination process as well as recent IRS policy changes could decrease the number of CNC accounts and increase collections of delinquent taxes.

Recommendations

In addition to our prior recommendation that local CNC postreview results be systematically collected and analyzed, we recommend that the Commissioner of Internal Revenue

- reinforce with supervisors and postreviewers the need to thoroughly review CNC determinations,
- establish processes that will ensure that the proper number of CNC postreviews are thoroughly done, and
- establish requirements for postreview reports that will ensure that they provide meaningful information that can be used in determining whether changes are needed.

Agency Comments and Our Evaluation

The Commissioner agreed with our recommendations to improve IRS' oversight of the CNC program. The Commissioner stated that IRS was exploring alternatives to remove various routine and administrative tasks from the managers' duties to allow them to concentrate on their core responsibilities, including the review of CNC accounts. CNC postreviews will be part of a combined Postreview/Collection Quality Management process located in regional sites. According to the Commissioner, this will eliminate any problems caused by conflicting demands. Also, because this is the primary activity of the review site, proper samples for CNC postreview are expected to be consistently achieved. The Commissioner also stated that the proposed review checklists for the consolidated postreview contain elements that can be analyzed to identify systemic issues and needed procedural changes.

Sampling and Data Analysis Methodology

As a part of our audit work, we reviewed the case files of a sample of individual taxpayer CNC accounts. Our sampling methodology enabled us to estimate parameters of the universe from which the sample was selected.

Sample Selection and Scope

We selected a stratified random sample of 107 individual taxpayer accounts from the accounts that were classified during August and September 1991 in 5 IRS district offices as CNC because of the taxpayer's financial hardship or because IRS was unable to locate or contact the taxpayer. The accounts were stratified by location and the reason for the CNC classification. Table I.1 shows the universe and sample sizes for each of the strata.

Table I.1: Sample Design for August-September 1991 Individual Taxpayer CNC Accounts

District Office	CNC classification	Universe size	Sample size
Albany	Unable to locate	8	5
	Unable to contact	1	1
	Unable to pay	98	14
Brooklyn	Unable to locate	55	6
	Unable to contact	53	5
	Unable to pay	269	9
Chicago	Unable to locate	35	5
	Unable to contact	47	5
	Unable to pay	98	10
Greensboro	Unable to locate	40	5
	Unable to contact	9	5
	Unable to pay	381	15
San Jose	Unable to locate	27	5
	Unable to contact	9	5
	Unable to pay	103	12

Sampling Errors for Individual Taxpayer CNC Accounts

Because we reviewed a statistical sample of individual taxpayer CNC accounts, each estimate developed from the sample has measurable sampling error, which is defined as the maximum amount by which the estimate obtained from a statistical sample can be expected to differ from the true universe value. The sampling error is used to develop a range, the lower limit of which is the estimate less the sampling error and the upper limit the estimate plus the sampling error. The sampling error, and therefore the magnitude of the range, resulting from a particular sample design also depends on how certain we want to be that the true universe parameter falls within this range. The degree of certainty we want is referred to as the confidence level, and the range is called the confidence interval.

For this report, we have selected a 95-percent confidence level. This means the chances are 19 out of 20 that if we reviewed all the individual taxpayer accounts that were classified during August and September 1991 at the 5 IRS district offices as CNC because of the taxpayer's financial hardship or because IRS was unable to locate or contact the taxpayer, the results of our review would differ from the estimates obtained from our sample by less than the sampling errors of such estimates. Table I.2 shows the upper and lower limits of the confidence intervals of key estimates used in the report.

Table I.2: Confidence Intervals for Key Universe Estimates, August-September 1991 Sample

		95-percent confidence interval	
Description	**Key estimates**	**Lower limit**	**Upper limit**
All CNC accounts			
Couples with joint liability filing separately	11.7%	4.2%	19.2%
CNC determination was questionable or inadequate	55.0%	44.0%	66.0%
Copies of lien documents were not in files	38.4%	26.8%	50.0%
Taxes owed in cases GAO found CNC determination was questionable or inadequate (in millions)	$30.7	$14.8	$46.7
Liens required to be filed	90.4%	84.0%	96.9%
Unable to pay accounts			
Future collection potential was not adequately considered	21.6%	10.0%	33.3%
Questionable living expenses were allowed	11.6%	3.3%	19.9%
Collection potential from assets was not fully considered	12.8%	4.9%	20.7%
Closing codes were set too high	19.8%	8.4%	31.2%

IRS Form 53

Report of Currently Not Collectible Taxes

1. Name and latest address of taxpayer *(underline name control)*

2. Schedule or transmittal

3. Notice of Lien filed ☐ Yes ☐ No

4. Form 53 charged out to

5. Name, SSN and home address of person(s) subject to TC 130 *(sole proprietor, partner, etc.)*
a. SSN:
b. SSN:

6. TC 130	Yes	No
a. Refund offset		
(1) Requested before	☐	☐
(2) Input required	☐	☐
b. Input on IMF to reactivate BMF CNC	☐	☐

7. Follow-up for	Yes	No
a. lien refile and/or waiver	☐	☐
b. other	☐	☐

8. Date of full compliance

9. Date of dr. *(cc 08)*

10. Should all BMF filing requirements be closed?	Yes	No
	☐	☐

11. Closed by

12. Location Code

13. TC **530**

14. Closing Code

15. Records/Sources Checked

Item	Date(s)
a. Directories	
b. Former employer	
c. Closed TDA and 53 file	
d. Postal service	
e. Neighbors	
f. Schools	
g. Personal property	
h. Vehicle registration	
i. Real property	
j. State employment	
k. Income tax return	

16. Description of Accounts

Taxpayer ID Number *(a)*	MFT Code *(b)*	Tax Period *(c)*	Cur. Not Collectible Assessed Balance *(d)*	Accrual Only *(e)*
		Total ▶		

17. Signature of originator

18. Date

19. Signature/title of approving manager

20. Date

21. Proposed Action	N/A	Date Submitted	Proposed Action	N/A	Date Submitted
a. 100% penalty assessment			c. Suit to reduce tax claim to judgment		
b. Transferee assessment			d. Proof of claim — Docket number		

22. Mandatory Follow-up Action	Date Required	Requested by	Date Completed	Completed by

Form **53** (Rev. 7-87) Part 1 Department of the Treasury Internal Revenue Service

Review *(Complete applicable blocks)*

☐ a. Letters 728(DO) or 728(C) not required

☐ b. Letters 728(DO) or 728(C) mailed ______________ *(Dates)*

☐ c. Reply attached

☐ d. No reply

☐ e. Returned undelivered

f. Status

☐ Approved *(after post review)*

☐ Rejected

g. Signature of Reviewing Officer

h. Date

MFT Codes and Type of Tax

01	Form 941 *(Withholding and FICA Taxes)*
02	Form 1120 *(Corporation Income Tax)*
03	Form 720 *(Excise Tax)*
09	Form CT-1 *(Railroad Retirement Tax)*
10	Form 940 *(FUTA Tax)*
30	Forms 1040, 1040A, and 1040-EZ *(Individual Income Tax)*

Closing Codes

03	Unable to locate
04	Statute expired prior to issuance
05	Statutory collection period expired after issuance or suit initiated to reduce tax claim to judgment
07	Bankrupt
08	Decedent case
09	Tolerance case
10	Defunct, insolvent corporation
12	Unable to contact
13	In-business corporation

Unable to pay: Follow-up and reissue TDA's if TPI of a subsequently filed return is more than any of the following amounts:

Code	Amount
24	$ 6,000
25	$ 9,000
26	$12,000
27	$15,000
28	$18,000
29	$21,000
30	$24,000
31	$27,000
32	$30,000

Codes 03, 12, and 24—32: There is no systemic reissuance of NMF accounts based on IMF filing. If a NMF account is currently not collectible under these codes and a follow-up is desirable, indicate this in Item 22.

Form **53** (Rev. 7-87)

Comments From the Internal Revenue Service

DEPARTMENT OF THE TREASURY
INTERNAL REVENUE SERVICE
WASHINGTON, D.C. 20224

COMMISSIONER

AUG 5 1993

Mr. Johnny C. Finch
Assistant Comptroller General
United States General Accounting Office
Washington, DC 20548

Dear Mr. Finch:

Thank you for the opportunity to review the draft report entitled "Tax Administration: IRS Can Do More to Collect Currently Not Collectible Tax Debts" (GAO/GGD-93-114).

We agree that this area can be improved and generally concur with the report recommendations. For some recommendations, we suggest alternative means of achieving these goals which more accurately reflect the requirements of administering a national program.

Also, I would like to take this opportunity to provide you with an update to page 38 of chapter 4 of your report. The profiling initiative mentioned in this chapter is still in the planning stage. The project is dependent upon better information to identify principal industrial activity and principal business activity. Discussions are in process with the Social Security Administration to secure this data. In any event, we expect this initiative will be more useful in refining our payroll tax delinquency identification and processing than the individual accounts which are the focus of this report.

We have enclosed our responses to the General Accounting Office's ten specific recommendations. We believe these responses accurately indicate the significant steps we have taken to date, and our plans to improve our Currently Not Collectible program.

Sincerely,

for Margaret Milner Richardson

Enclosure

IRS COMMENTS ON GAO DRAFT REPORT ENTITLED
"TAX ADMINISTRATION: IRS CAN DO MORE TO COLLECT
CURRENTLY NOT COLLECTIBLE TAX DEBTS"

Recommendation #1: The Commissioner should establish specific guidelines for determining taxpayer ability to pay delinquent taxes, including criteria for determining dollar ranges for reasonable and necessary expenses.

The Service has wrestled with this issue for a number of years. The broad guidelines contained in the Internal Revenue Manual are a response to concerns that nationally mandated ranges for reasonable and necessary expenses must be quite broad to accommodate differences in local cost of living. For example, a housing allowance range which allows for the variance in the rental market between a low cost rural area and a major metropolis is unlikely to offer specific guidance for our employees making these decisions.

We feel that one practical method of approaching this problem is to consult with other agencies responsible for management and collection of Federal debt; for example, the student loan program and various secured mortgage programs. This information, in conjunction with data from sources such as the Department of Labor, could be used as a framework for general guidelines. It would be reasonable, for instance, to expect that a taxpayer in the upper five percent of family income will at least make payments to resolve their tax debt.

These guidelines would still require local consultation of such sources as local consumer price index information for housing, food, and other living expenses. In addition, the Internal Revenue Manual will be revised to emphasize that items which are lifestyle choices, such as ownership or lease of luxury automobiles, private education, luxury housing, and similar items do not constitute hardship issues for determining ability to pay. While the IRS will not dictate lifestyle choices to a taxpayer, the expectation will exist that high income taxpayers are expected to make the choices neccessary to resolve their tax obligations. Our personnel will use their financial analysis skills to assist taxpayers in this process.

These actions are a long term commitment to improvement of the quality of Currently Not Collectible accounts. We will be contacting other agencies to determine how they approach these problems. As this is a substantial departure from our usual method of operations, we feel the involvement of Collection executives and top level management is essential to ensure these changes are accepted in our front line operations.

Recommendation #2: The Commissioner should establish specific guidelines for selecting an income level at which unable to pay CNC accounts will be reactivated.

We agree with this recommendation and will include specific language in the next revision of the relevant portions of the Internal Revenue Manual.

Recommendation #3: The Commissioner should require, except in extraordinary situations, at least minimum payments from delinquent taxpayers with incomes above a specified level.

We agree with this recommendation in principle. Rather than specifying an income level, we will emphasize through additional Internal Revenue Manual guidelines that the determination of the hardship condition does not include items which are lifestyle choices as noted above. Where such choices limit the ability of the taxpayer to pay the tax debt, at least minimum payments will be made. The disallowance of personal choice items is an issue which will vary on a case by case basis. Also, the absence of distrainable assets is a factor in many CNC determinations.

Recommendation #4: The Commissioner should eliminate the automatic 65-week reactivation hold period and allow employees to determine when CNC accounts should be considered for reactivation purposes.

We do not agree with this recommendation. National Office discussions with General Accounting Office personnel indicated that the reactivation hold exists for sound administrative reasons. The 65-week hold prevents reactivation of a case based on income information which has already been considered. If a thorough investigation is conducted, financial information analyzed for disposition of the case will reflect the income reported on the current year income tax return. If that income figure is adequate to generate reactivation, the account should not be reported CNC. Refinements of the decision process noted in the responses to Recommendations 1-3 should rectify these situations. The mandatory follow-up option is also available to address situations where short term improvement in financial condition occurs. The elimination of the automatic hold would result in unnecessary reactivations and poor use of resources when alternatives exist to address these concerns.

Recommendation #5: The Commissioner should track both taxpayers with joint delinquencies to ensure that each taxpayer's ability to pay or status is considered in the reactivation decision.

We agree with this recommendation in principle. However, the individual master file, as it presently exists, does not have the ability to track the payment potential or update the status of the secondary party to a joint entity. As noted in the body of the report, we have indicated our readiness to pursue this issue as an element of Tax Systems Modernization.

Recommendation #6: The Commissioner should use all pertinent available indicators of collection potential as reactivation criteria.

While we agree with the principle expressed in this recommendation, the case examples cited do not contain sufficient detail for us to determine whether the issues noted relate to weaknesses in the CNC determination process or other factors. The examples cited note significant interest or dividend income from underlying assets or proceeds of sale of long-term assets. These reviews were conducted for 1990 returns for recent CNC determinations. The interest may well have been generated on bank accounts levied prior to the CNC action. The long term asset gain could conceivably have been the result of our own distraint action or forced liquidation to partially satisfy the liability. If the examples represent genuine shortcomings in the investigations, corrective actions should address the failure to identify the underlying assets. The issue is not one of reactivation criteria.

Recommendation #7: The Commissioner should expedite the processing of reactivated cases by reducing the number of notices and making prior case files readily available for IRS employees working reactivated cases.

We agree there may be benefits in reducing the number of notices sent to reactivated CNC cases and assigning the accounts to the Collection function. The prior case files can be of great benefit to an employee working a reactivated case to establish a taxpayer's "track record" or search for inconsistencies in the current financial data and that gleaned in a prior investigation.

These files should be available from the Federal Records Center but are not requested for routine association with reactivated case files generated in the IRS service centers. The files should be requested by the investigating employees as needed. The Assistant Commissioner (Collection) will determine if field offices are experiencing difficulties with these requests.

Recommendation #8: The Commissioner should reinforce with supervisors and post reviewers the need to thoroughly review CNC determinations.

We agree that managers should exercise their review responsibilities conscientiously. Currently, we are exploring alternatives to remove various routine and administrative tasks from managers' duties to allow them the time and flexibility to concentrate on their core responsibilities, including the review of CNC accounts. We feel the answer lies, at least partially, in allowing managers the flexibility to concentrate their review efforts in areas where there are known weaknesses in investigative techniques. Our first line managers are the key to development of our employees and improvement of quality.

National Office reviews of the post review activity have indicated that the quality of post reviews improve in centralized review sites. Cases are reviewed from a consistent perspective and the activity is perceived as central to the function of the centralized site. District post review activity tends to be located in the Special Procedures function (SPf) and can be adversely affected by the demands of bankruptcy and other litigation activity demands on limited staffpower.

Recommendation #9: The Commissioner should establish processes that will ensure that the proper number of CNC post reviews are thoroughly done.

We agree with the recommendation. In response to an earlier GAO recommendation that we accumulate post review results at the national level, we are working on the implementation of a combined Post Review/Collection Quality Management System process in the existing regional sites. As the primary activity of the review site, we expect the samples for CNC post review will be achieved in a consistent fashion. As noted above, our district post review activities sometimes suffer due to the competition of high priority bankruptcy and litigation work in the district SPf.

Recommendation #10: The Commissioner should establish processes that will ensure that they provide meaningful information that can be used in determining whether changes are needed.

The review checklists proposed for consolidated post review contain a list of core elements specific to the appropriateness and quality of the CNC determination. These elements will provide the data for a national report which can be analyzed to identify systemic issues and needed procedural changes.

Major Contributors to This Report

General Government Division, Washington, D.C.

Cornelia M. Blanchette, Assistant Director, Tax Policy and Administration Issues
Robert J. McArter, Assistant Director, Tax Policy and Administration Issues
Charlie W. Daniel, Assignment Manager

Chicago Regional Office

Thomas D. Venezia, Regional Management Representative
Dan Meyer, Evaluator-in-Charge
Gail F. Marnik, Site Senior
Delano B. Pulido, Evaluator
Francis M. Zbylski, Senior Operations Research Analyst